The Mystery of Godliness

I0164895

Glen Burch

ISBN: 978-1-78364-488-9

www.obt.org.uk

Scripture quotations are primarily the author's own translation. Others use the *King James Version (KJV)* or *New KJV (NKJV)*.

Some Scripture quotations are from The Authorized (King James) Version. Rights in the Authorized Version in the United Kingdom are vested in the Crown. Reproduced by permission of the Crown's patentee, Cambridge University Press.

****

The Open Bible Trust
Fordland Mount, Upper Basildon,
Reading, RG8 8LU, UK.

The Mystery of Godliness

Contents

Page

Introduction

Introduction

Of all the doctrines that we adhere to as Christians certainly one of the most essential is the fact that Jesus Christ is truly God. In our search for a Scriptural expression of this great foundational truth, many of us have turned to the eloquent phrase "the mystery of godliness" in Paul's first letter to Timothy. The passage containing this phrase is all the more effective for its simplicity of expression. The KJV renders 1 Timothy 3:16 thus:

> And without controversy great is the mystery of godliness: God was manifest in the flesh, justified in the Spirit, seen of angels, preached unto the Gentiles, believed on in the world, received up into glory.

Commentators have long noted the lyrical quality of the verse, suggesting that it may have served as an early Christian hymn or lesson (like the five "faithful sayings" in the Pastoral Epistles[1]). But

---

[1] 1 Timothy 1:15; 3:1; 4:9; 2 Timothy 2:11; Titus 3:8

the text offers no clue as having been a quote from another source, and we may conclude that it was uniquely Paul's mission to reveal the mystery of godliness.

At first glance the passage does seem to display an unambiguous witness to the deity of Christ. "God was manifest in the flesh" seems plain enough. However, upon closer examination questions arise. For example, take the Greek words for "godliness" (*eusebeia*) and "godly" (*eusebōs*). Although rendered "piety", "devout" and "holiness" elsewhere, none of these words fully expresses the meaning of *eusebeia*, which derives from *eu* (well) and *sebomai* (worship).

The root meaning is one of reverence and worship that is well-pleasing to God. The English "godliness" can be a misleading rendering of *eusebeia* because it seems to imply "Godlikeness", and this connotation is off the mark. But this is necessarily the sense that we read into "godliness" if we use "the mystery of godliness" as a proof text for the deity of Christ.

Although Christ is described as having "godly fear" (NKJV – Hebrews 5:7) in His prayers at Gethsemane, the Holy Spirit was careful to use another word here. *Eulabeia* has a root meaning of taking heed or using caution, as in the LXX of Leviticus 15:31, and a derivative meaning of piety or reverence, which is its meaning in modern Greek. But for all the humble exampleship of His life, including prayer, the record does not describe Jesus as having *eusebeia*.

Nonetheless, to follow Christ's example of lowliness and prayerful obedience to the Father would certainly lead us into a godly life. "Godliness" is not the imitation of God's character, although such imitation is required of us ("become imitators of God as beloved children" – Ephesians 5:1). Rather, it expresses the desire to worship Him aright. And the Scriptures stop short of describing the Son as worshipping the Father. If the mystery of godliness has to do with the Person of Christ, and *eusebeia* has its normal meaning, it would rather demean His deity to my thinking.

A further difficulty with the popular interpretation

of the mystery of godliness is its irrelevance to the context of 1 Timothy 3. The immediate context is in verses 14 and 15:

> These things I write to you, hoping to come to you quickly. But if I should be delayed, so that you may know how you ought to conduct yourself in God's house, which is *the* Living God's church, a column and base of the truth.

This is followed by the conclusion in verse 16:

> And confessedly great is the mystery of godliness: God was manifested in flesh, was justified in spirit, appeared to angels, was proclaimed among nations, was believed in *the* world, was taken up in glory.

How might the presumed incarnation ("manifested in flesh"), the baptism ("justified in, or by, Spirit"), the redemptive work (as "seen by angels, proclaimed among nations, believed in the world"), or the ascension ("taken up in glory") of Jesus serve as an example to Timothy in his conduct in the church? If "the mystery of godliness" describes Jesus' incarnation, work of redemption, and ascension, it is mostly beyond our reach to emulate. And the "so that you may know how you ought to conduct yourself" would be out of place.

Other difficulties have to do with the six items delineating the mystery of godliness. If this is a synopsis of the earthly sojourn of Christ, then how could this mystery have already been "proclaimed among nations" before the ascension? This pronouncement of non-Israelite blessing is all the more remarkable because the Jew is not even mentioned. It is as if the covenant-people did not exist!

Further, how does "appeared to angels" fit into the earthly life of Jesus? How did the stewardship of angels accord with God's covenant plan? And how with the dispensation of the mystery? The theme of angelic participation in the spiritual affairs of men will be more fully explored in the next chapter.

The purpose of this study is to demonstrate how

the mystery of godliness harmonizes better when aligned with the mystery that distinguishes our heavenly hope today. Paul's Epistle to the Ephesians is more explicit than 1 Timothy in its teaching on the mystery of our church:

Because of this, I Paul, the prisoner of Christ Jesus for you the nations – seeing that you gave heed to the dispensation of the grace of God, which was given to me for you, that according to revelation He made known to me **the mystery**, according as I wrote before in brief, for which (mystery) reading *it* you are able to understand my comprehension in **the mystery of Christ**, which (mystery) to other generations was not made known to the sons of mankind, as it was now revealed to His holy apostles and prophets in spirit - the nations to be joint-heirs and joint-bodies and joint-sharers of the promise in Christ Jesus through the gospel, of which I became minister according to the gift of the grace of God which was given to me according to the in-working of His power, to me the less-than-least of all holy ones was given this grace to preach to the nations the untraceable wealth of the Christ, and to enlighten all *to* what *is* **the dispensation of the mystery**, which has been hidden from the ages by the *same* God Who created all these things. (Ephesians 3:1-9)

This is one of several passages in Ephesians and Colossians which deal with a unique revelation, "the mystery", revealed to Paul during his ministry from prison. That mystery concerns the founding of a new church, which is extra-national in membership and heavenly in hope. The earthly kingdom, with Israel at its center, was postponed at the end of Acts. Since that time, a new dispensation has been in operation, and the offer of every spiritual blessing in the heavenlies in Christ (Ephesians 1:3) has gone out to mankind, regardless of race or nation. But note the emphasis above "to preach to the nations" – again Israel is not central to this preaching. This mystery had been kept secret since the foundation of the world.

The distinctive viewpoint of "the mystery" as found in 1 Timothy 3 is the power that Christ our Head has worked into His church, the body in which His fullness has come to dwell (Ephesians 1:23). Individual members endowed with this fullness are enabled to work out their salvation in lives of faith. Verse 16 summarizes under the heading, "mystery of godliness", the whole issue of godly conduct which so dominates the Pastoral Epistles – 1 and 2 Timothy, and Titus.

The Mystery of Christ

The Mystery of Christ

In order to develop a better interpretation of the mystery of godliness, we must first build a doctrinal framework based on "the mystery of Christ". This will only be a cursory look at the mystery of Christ. Where it relates to salvation in general, the mystery of Christ can be found in almost every quarter of the Scriptures, for they all speak of Him (John 5:39). We have today the twin advantages of a completed canon and spiritual insight into all its "secrets" ("secret" is a more accurate rendering of the Greek *mustērion*, often translated "mystery").

This is not to presume that men have fully understood all the truth about the Christ. Much about His first advent was only hinted at in the types, shadows and prophecies of the Old Testament. The depth of Who Christ was and what His work accomplished were kept back by God until the proper time to reveal it. The full revelation concerning Christ and His new-covenant sacrifice at Calvary, being spiritual in nature, was withheld until after His resurrection.

Afterwards, the ascended Lord sent another Teacher, the Holy Spirit, to lead believers of the Acts period into the covenant mysteries of the Christ (John 14:25-26; 16:12-14; 1 John 2:20, 27). Paul touched upon the revelation of this truth at the end of Romans:

> But to Him Who can strengthen you, according to my gospel even the proclamation of Jesus Christ, according to *the* revelation of **a mystery** having been silenced for age-times, but now having been manifested and, through *the* prophetic Scriptures, having been made known for faith-obedience for all the nations according to *the* command of the eternal God Romans 16:25-26

Here we find an aspect of the mystery of Christ that was both manifested through the prophetic Scriptures and hidden there. The mystery revealed in Romans concerns:

a) Christ as the Second Adam, Heir of a redeemed race of men (Romans 5).

b) The believer's identification with the work of Christ and the spiritual consequences of this (Romans 6).

c) The temporary failure of Israel to receive their Messiah, and the grafting of the nations into Israel's blessings – a hidden fulfillment of God's promise to Abram in Genesis 12:3 (Romans 9-11).

A very different aspect of the mystery of Christ meets us in the Scriptures of Paul's prison ministry. Although it shares some fundamental truths with Romans 5-8, this mystery was NOT the subject of previous Scripture.

> that according to revelation He made known to me **the mystery**, according as I wrote before briefly, for sake of which you are able, reading *it*, to perceive my understanding in **the mystery of the Christ**, which (mystery) in other generations was not made known to the sons of men as it has now been revealed to His holy apostles and prophets by the Spirit. (Ephesians 3:3-5)

of which I became a minister according to the dispensation of God which was given to me for you to complete the word of God, **the mystery** which has been hidden from the ages and the generations, but now was manifested to His holy ones. (Colossians 1:25-26)

Besides the utter secrecy concerning it, this new element of the mystery of Christ is characterized by two things:

a) A hope declared to all nations without distinction (i.e., the Jew no longer first; Abraham no longer the channel of blessing).

b) A church with a heavenly destiny – not in the heavenly Jerusalem, but in Christ at the Father's right hand.

These truths stand out as unique to Paul's prison ministry, differing from his covenant-based Acts period message.

The Place of the Gentile in God's Promises.

Jesus Christ, "minster of the circumcision" (Romans 15:8), was "not sent except unto the lost sheep of *the* house of Israel" (Matthew 15:24). At first, He also restricted His apostles:

> Go not into *the* way of nations and enter not into a city of Samaritans, but journey rather to the lost sheep of *the* house of Israel. And journeying, proclaim, saying, 'The kingdom of the heavens has drawn near.'(Matthew 10:5-7)

At that time Gentiles were looked upon as "dogs" dispensationally, fit only to receive crumbs from the Master's table (Matthew 15:21-27). It should be clear that neither the Lord nor His disciples "proclaimed unto the nations" (fourth element of the mystery of godliness) during Jesus' stay on earth. Following His resurrection, Jesus modified the Matthew 10 command:

> Journeying into the whole world, proclaim the gospel to the whole creation. (Mark 16:15)

But who was meant by "the whole creation"? Only *after* the Pentecostal endowment of holy spirit, did the Twelve venture into Samaritan towns and the byways of the nations, preaching to the twelve tribes only (James 1:1; 1 Peter 1:1). Had Israel repented at their preaching, the Lord would have returned to restore kingdom glory to Israel and David's throne in Jerusalem (Acts 1:6; 3:19-21).

The only Gentiles to receive the gospel from the Twelve were the household of the centurion Cornelius in Acts 10. This was a unique exception for Peter (the apostle of the circumcision – Galatians 2:8), like Jesus granting the request of the Canaanite woman (Matthew 15:28). But Cornelius himself was a special case, being a "God-fearer" (Acts 10:2), i.e. just short of being a Jewish proselyte. Cornelius' call followed the Great Pentecost by eight years.

This lone convert of Peter's outside his own nation followed a time of poor harvest among the sons of Israel. The Gentile was becoming a means to provoking Israel to jealousy (Romans 11:13-14).

Before Cornelius, the kingdom was being offered to the Jew only, and after him to the Jew first – via Paul, Barnabas and their affiliated ministry.

When Paul appears on the scene, we find him persecuting the church (entirely Jewish) "into the way of the Gentiles" (Acts 26:11-12). This "chosen vessel" was to receive on-going instruction in his ministry:

> … for this *reason* I (Jesus) appeared to you, to appoint you for Myself a helper and a witness both of what you saw and of what I will appear to you *concerning*, rescuing you from the People and from the nations, unto whom I am sending you. (Acts 26:16-17)

In his seven Epistles written during Acts (Romans, 1 and 2 Corinthians, Galatians, 1 and 2 Thessalonians, and Hebrews) and throughout the book of Acts itself, we find Paul preaching "to the Jew first and also the Greek" (Romans 1:16). This fulfilled the first part of his apostolic appointment. At that time salvation was "of the Jews" (John 4:22) and by Paul's apostleship a Gentile company was brought in for Israel's sake, "to provoke them to jealousy" (Romans 11:11). These Gentiles were like branches of "a wild olive tree … grafted contrary to nature into a cultivated olive tree", which was Israel (Romans 11:17-24). The late crisis of disbelief by Roman Jews (Acts 28:23-27) was a turning point for Israel, although Paul continued another two years with his Acts period ministry. The judgment of Isaiah 6:9-10 was pronounced then for the last time, but as ever the Lord was slow in fulfilling His threat. What remained a close secret was what God would do if Israel failed.

And what God did was totally unexpected. The Abrahamic and Mosaic covenants were set aside for a time, and a new blessing was revealed for all mankind, regardless of nation. This is the subject of Paul's last seven Epistles – principally Ephesians and Colossians (also Philippians, 1 and 2 Timothy, Titus, and Philemon). In them he teaches various aspects of this "dispensation of the grace of God" (Ephesians 3:2) – both doctrinal and practical. Here Paul describes himself as "the prisoner of Jesus Christ for you nations"

(Ephesians 3:1 - Israelites included). Note that *ethnos* means "nation", and we should be wary of translating it as "Gentile" to the exclusion of Israel. In fact *ethnos* is used of Judea/Israel 14 times in the NT, and of Samaria once. It is best to think of "the nations" during this dispensation of grace as "all mankind". Ephesians 2:11-13 does distinguish "the nations in the flesh" (uncircumcision) from the circumcision (Jewish nation) in the former dispensation. However, that fleshly distinction has been wiped out in this dispensation, and concerning the "one new man" it says:

...where there is within neither Greek nor Jew, circumcision nor uncircumcision. (Colossians 3:11)

A brand new ultra-national mankind has replaced the old national distinctions in the church today.

The Role of the Elect Angels

The involvement of the elect angels in the present aspect of God's purpose of the ages appears to be a passive one:

> To me, the least than least of all holy ones was given this grace to preach to the nations the untraceable wealth of the Christ, and to enlighten all *as to* what *is* the dispensation of the mystery, which has been hidden from the ages in the *same* God Who created all these things, so that now to the principalities and authorities in the heavenlies might be made known through the church the multifarious wisdom of God, according to the purpose of the ages which He accomplished by Christ Jesus our Lord. (Ephesians 3:8-11)

Note how Paul's mission "to preach to the nations" this "dispensation of the mystery" sounds remarkably like the fourth element of the mystery of godliness. The point in the passage above is that spiritual powers in heaven are getting an object-lesson by observing Christ the Head operating in the church which is His body (Ephesians 1:22-23). Apart from this, there appears to be no angelic participation with men in the heavenly kingdom of Christ – at least for the present time.

Angelic passivity is a dramatic change from their prior and future roles in the outworking of the covenants and God's earthly plan. In every age but the present one God uses His angels as instruments of judgment on earth (Hebrews 1:7). The blasting of Sodom and Gomorra, the plagues on Egypt, and the final woes upon the earth in the day of the Lord are all part of this angelic ministry. The covenant of the Law with Israel was administered by angels (Hebrews 1:13-14; 2:2), who communicated His word to men and resisted demonic powers (Daniel 10:5-14).

In contrast, during this "dispensation of the grace of God" divine judgment remains suspended. A church filled up with the fullness of Christ (Ephesian 1:22-23), which has received the completed word of God (Colossians 1:25), has no need of angelic messengers. Neither is there any basis in the rightly divided Scriptures for believing that angels are now contending with devils, as when Michael disputed with Satan over the body of Moses (Jude 9).

Our only contact with angels today involves the

spiritual contest which pits the church "against the world-rulers of this darkness" (Ephesians 6:12). The angelic armies who are loyal to God appear to be resting, as it were, held in reserve for the great battle of the day of the Lord. This contrast between the activities of the elect and fallen angels may be observed in the central section of 1 Timothy, separated by only a "but" in 4:1.

Here we find a sharp distinction between the mystery of godliness as passively "seen by angels" (3:16) and the ongoing mystery of iniquity practiced by "deceiving spirits and teachings of demons" (4:2). Angelic messages received in the present dispensation should be rejected by the faithful as "teachings of demons". For a believer today to seek any relationship with angels, other than that revealed in Ephesians 3:10-11, is to depart from "the sound teaching".

The Doctrine
of
Godliness

The Doctrine of Godliness

A godly manner of life is the subject of much teaching in the Pastoral Epistles, and a concordance of the various "godly" words will show the extent of this.

The noun "godliness" – *eusebeia* (only five occurrences outside the Pastoral Epistles, but ten within).

> … that we may lead a quiet and peaceful life in all **godliness** and dignity. (1 Timothy 2:2)

> … that you may know how you ought to conduct yourself in God's house, which is Living God's church … confessedly great is the mystery of **godliness** ... (1 Timothy 3:16)

> … exercise yourself toward **godliness**. For the bodily exercise is profitable for a little *while*, but the **godliness** is profitable for all things, having a promise of life that *is* now, and that *is*

coming. (1 Timothy 4:7-8)

if anyone teaches otherwise and agrees not to sound words, which *are* of our Lord Jesus Christ, even to the teaching according to **godliness**, he has been puffed up, understanding nothing, but being sick about debates and word-battles, from which come envy, strife, evil speaking, evil suspicions, constant argumentations of men having been corrupted in the mind and having been defrauded of the truth, supposing **godliness** to be gain, but **godliness** with satisfaction is great gain. (1 Timothy 6:3-6)

But you, O man of God, flee these things and pursue righteousness, **godliness**, faith, love, perseverance, gentleness. (1 Timothy 6:11)

But come to know this: in last days hard times will be present, for men will be lovers of self, lovers of money, boasters, arrogant, slanderers, rebellious to parents, ungrateful, impious, inhuman, irreconcilable, gossips, uncontrolled, vicious, not loving good, traitors, reckless, puffed up, loving pleasure rather than loving God, holding to a form of **godliness** but denying its power – even avoid these ones. (2 Timothy 3:1-5)

Paul, slave of God ... according to *the* faith of God's chosen and *the* acknowledgement of truth that *is* according to **godliness** ... (Titus 1:1)

The adverb "godly" – *eusebōs* (only in the Pastorals).

And all who *are* desiring to live **godly** in Christ Jesus will be pressed. (2 Timothy 3:12)

... disciplining us that denying the ungodliness and the worldly passions, we should live sound-mindedly and righteously and **godly** in the present age. (Titus 2:12)

The adjective "godly" – *eusebēs* (not in the Pastorals, but has 3 NT occurrences).

The verb "to be godly" – *eusebeō*.

But if any widow has children or grandchildren, let them learn first **to be godly** to their own house and to give back repayment to the parents, for this is pleasing before God.   (1 Timothy 5:4)

In its only other NT occurrence *eusebeō* must be rendered "worship":

... for passing by and reflecting upon your objects of worship (*sebasmata* – derived from *sebomai*, a root of *eusebeia*), I even found an altar with the inscription: 'To a god unknown.' Whom, therefore, you **worship** being in ignorance, This One I proclaim to you. (Acts 17:23)

Summing up from the Pastorals, godliness is:

1) The means to leading a quiet, peaceful life
2) The secret of this kind of life shows how to conduct oneself in the church
3) The profitable goal of spiritual exercise
4) The sound words of Jesus Christ - the godliness doctrine

5) The pursuit of a man of God
6) A powerless counterfeit of godliness will be practiced in last days
7) Godliness truth is acknowledged by the faithful chosen
8) A desirable way to live
9) Practical home-life, and the proper care of one's parents

Clearly the doctrine of godliness, or piety, is a major theme in the Pastoral Epistles. None of the relevant texts, except perhaps 1 Timothy 3:16, deals with the Person of Christ directly, and in the last text above the meaning of "worship" in godliness is very clear. Godliness appears to be the worshipful attitude in a Christian that affects every detail of his daily walk. In a sense, a believer's manner of life **IS** his worship. Furthermore, there is no prescription today for an outward, formalistic, or priestly mode of worship. That type of worship passed off the scene with the interruption of Israel's laws and covenants. Godliness is the quintessence of spiritual worship.

The True Worship

Those who would worship God well in this dispensation must do so in spirit, because the ritualistic elements ("rudiments" in the KJV of Colossians 2:8 and 20-23) of Judaic worship are inappropriate for the present.

> Beware the dogs. Beware the evil workers. Beware the mutilation! For we are the circumcision who *are* serving God in spirit and boasting in Christ Jesus and not having trusted in flesh. (Philippians 3:2-3)

> For He is our peace Who made the both one and destroyed the dividing-wall of the fence, the hatred in His flesh, having abolished the law of commandments in regulations, so that He might create in Himself the two into one new man, making peace. (Ephesians 2:14-15)

This was no longer the voice of one bound "for the hope of Israel" (Acts 28:20), who "to the Jews became as a Jew" (1 Corinthians 9:20; Romans 14:1-15:1). Man in the flesh is eager to perform outward religious works, but this cannot please the One Who has provided us our marching orders for this dispensation. Those who impose such religious schemes on others are characterized by the Holy Spirit as "dogs" and "evil workers". The language becomes even stronger toward the end of Philippians 3:

> Yet for what we achieved, *you are* to live by the same. Brothers become joint-imitators of me and mark those walking like this, just as you have us *as* a pattern. For many are walking, of whom I told you often, and now tell even weeping – **'the enemies of the cross of Christ'** – whose end *is* ruin, whose god *is* the belly and the glory in their shame, who *are* minding the earthly *things*. (Philippians 3:16-19)

This injunction against minding "the earthly things" is not a recommendation of the ascetic life. Neither does "the enemies of the cross of Christ" refer to the Jews who rejected Jesus. It does condemn Christians who become Judaized into holding a form of earthly hope and practicing an earthly worship (elements of Mosaic Law).

Blessings in the earth are a promise of the Abrahamic covenant (Genesis 12:1-3), the Mosaic covenant (Exodus 19:5-6), the Levitical covenant (Numbers 18:19-24), the Davidic covenant (2 Samuel 7:5-16), and the New covenant (Jeremiah 31:31-34; 32:37-44; Matthew 5:5). Even the heavenly city, New Jerusalem (Hebrews 3:1; 11:13-16; 12:22-24) appears not to bless the overcomers until it descends to the earth (Revelation 21:9-14). But the church of "the mystery" is blessed with every spiritual blessing in the heavenlies, and is entirely separate from earthly families (Genesis 12:1-3; Ephesians 3:15).

Warnings against an earthly form of worship are also found in the middle portion of Colossians. Chapter 2 begins with a personal, agonizing appeal from the apostle Paul:

> For I want you to know how great a struggle I have for you, and those at Laodicea and as many as have not seen my face in *the* flesh, so that their hearts might be encouraged, having been joined together in love and for all *the* wealth of the certainty of the understanding, for

the recognition of the mystery of God – Christ, in Whom are hidden all the treasures of the wisdom and knowledge. (Colossians 2:1-3)

The text continues with admonitions against "enticing words" (or 'attractive arguments' - v.4), "philosophy and empty deception", "the tradition of men", "the elements of the world" (v.8), "the hand-writing of the regulations" (v.14) concerning food and drink and keeping a religious calendar of feasts, new moons and sabbaths (v.16) – shadows all! Then verse 18 opens up the awful possibility of losing one's reward in connection with a "worshipping of angels". The verse reads:

Let no one rule (lit. 'umpire') against you, desiring by lowly-mindedness and religion of the angels what things he has seen, entering upon *them*, in vain puffed up by the mind of his flesh. (Colossians 2:18)

At issue is access into the heavenly Holy of Holies. In Christ the believer has this access guaranteed him (Ephesians 2:18), to the point of being reckoned by God as already seated there in

Glory (Ephesians 2:6). On the other hand, angels must take a place outside the curtain of the heavenly Holies, as no seating arrangement has been made for them within (Hebrews 1:13). Only a false humility can motivate us to remain outside with them in our worship. The worthiness to enter has been provided by Christ, in Whom the church was chosen "holy and faultless" (Ephesians 1:4).

Those who claim for their religious utterings the tongues of angels need to take this Colossians warning to heart, for the angels cannot mediate for us with God. Likewise the mediation of priests and preachers is wholly contrary to our completeness in Christ (Colossians 2:10). All is of His grace for us, and to shrink from these spiritual blessings is to take up commandments of men, subjecting ourselves to earthly ordinances (Colossians 2:20-22). We who have been baptized spiritually are commanded to put away all earthly forms of worship:

> If, therefore, you were raised with Christ, seek the things above where Christ is sitting at *the* right hand of God. Be minded on the things

above, not on the things regarding the earth. For you died and your life has been hidden with Christ in God. When Christ your life may appear, then also will you appear with Him in *the* Glory. (Colossians 3:1-4)

Not being mindful of "the things regarding the earth" cannot mean ignoring our bodily existence and earthly needs. That is asceticism, itself a fleshly human regulation. "The things regarding the earth" are its religious forms and worship.

The "Glory" in which the mystery church will be manifested with Christ is not the sky-glory of Christ as Priest-King of Israel. When the Son of David returns in splendor from heaven (Matthew 24:20-31; 1 Thessalonians 4:15-17), He will establish His kingdom on earth with Israel at its center. Neither is the heavenly glory of Colossians 3:4 to be confused with the later sky-glory of "the new heaven" when "New Jerusalem" descends out of the sky into the earth (Revelation 21:1-2). Our manifestation in Glory with Christ our Head is as un-seeable to us at present as Christ Himself (1 Timothy 6:16). For the present, we can spiritually begin to apprehend "the breadth and length and height and depth" of this future blessing. To partake of such a kingdom requires a greater degree of spirituality than was needed previously. Now it has become necessary to lay aside earthly modes of worship, which come naturally to us because of the flesh, and to find our *all* in Christ.

> … you are filled by Him Who is the Head of every principality and authority. (Colossians 2:10)

> … not holding fast the Head from Whom the whole body, by the ligaments and fastenings, being supplied and held together, grows the growth of God. (Colossians 2:19)

Our formula for a right walk is plainly revealed here. Holding fast our completeness in Christ at every turn in life is the godly life. This attitude of mind is suggested also by the context of the mystery of godliness, to which we must turn for closer study.

The Mystery of Godliness Re-Examined

The Mystery of Godliness Re-Examined

Allowing that *eusebeia* does not mean "Godlikeness", there are still multiple ways to take the expression "the mystery of godliness". For example, was Thayer correct in calling it "the mystery which is held by godliness and nourishes it" or "used generally, of Christian truth as hidden from ungodly men: with the addition of *tēs pisteōs*, *tēs eusebeias*, which faith and godliness embrace and keep, 1 Timothy iii.9, 16"?[2] H.K. Moulton reduces this mystery to "religion, the Christian religion".[3]

His father, J.H. Moulton, in researching the mundane meaning of NT words from non-literary Koine sources, observed an instance of the adverb

---

[2] *Greek-English Lexicon of the New Testament*, J.H. Thayer, p.262.
[3] *Analytical Greek Lexicon Revised*, H.K. Moulton, 1978 Edition, p.176.

eusebōs which must be translated "scrupulously".[4] Each of these observations may add to our insight, but for a reliable interpretation we must take up a thorough examination of the Biblical context. Before this, however, an issue of variant readings needs to be reviewed.

The ancient NT manuscripts and early Christian writers are not in agreement over the wording "*God* was manifested in the flesh..." in verse 16. The Companion Bible margin[5] comes to our aid with some history of this disputed reading:

> *God.* The R.V. prints "He Who", and adds in margin, "*Theos* (God) rests on no sufficient evidence". The probability is that the original reading was *ho* (which), with the Syriac and all the Latin versions, to agree with *mustērion* (neut.). The Gr. uncial being O, some scribe added the letter *s*, making OC (He Who), which he thought made better sense. Later another put a mark in this O, making ΘC, the contraction

---

[4] *Vocabulary of the Greek Testament*, Moulton and Milligan, p.266.

[5] *The Companion Bible*, E.W. Bullinger, p. 1803.

for ΘEOC, God. This mark in Codex A, in the British Museum, is said by some to be in different ink.

The text of Nestle-Aland 26th edition prefers the reading "which" over "God" based on a likely corruption due to the *nomina sacra* abbreviations. The following excerpt from Kurt and Barbara Aland's **The Text of the New Testament,** p.278 describes how this might have happened:

At the beginning of Acts 1:3, for example are the words *hois kai paresthsen.* Some manuscripts here read *o Iesous paresthsen ...* The words fit the context, but it is puzzling to us why the variant should have occurred until we remember that in the uncials the text could have been OIC, and that the nomina sacra were written in abbreviated form, with ΘC for *Theos,* KC for *Kurios,* IC for *Iesous.* Then it becomes clear that the scribe who wrote *ho Iesous* at Acts 1:3 was copying from an uncial exemplar in which a bar had inadvertently been placed over IC (as it actually happens in Codex Ephraemi Syri Rescriptus [C]). The error is obvious (and the variant is not noted in the apparatus of Nestle-Aland [26]). The reverse process may also occur, as in the hymn to Christ in 1 Tim. 3:16. The original reading here was *hos ephanerothe* (as in ℵ* A* C* F G 33 365 *pc*), i.e., in the uncial script ΟΣΕΦΑΝΕΡΩΘΗ. Only a stroke of the pen needed to be added above ΟΣ, and the misreading of ΟΣ as ΘΣ (*Theos*) was almost inevitable (in a single step), with an enhancement of devotional overtones. The correction was made accordingly by later hands in ℵ, A, and C: *Theos* is read by ℵ[C] A[C] C[C] D[2] Ψ *M* vg[ms], and in a further stage (in 88 *pc*) the article *ho* was added.

Whether we accept these judgments as probable, or not, the task of demonstrating that the Christ-indwelled church is the mystery of godliness does not depend on the use of a particular variant.

Our investigation will take us through contexts near and far in the Mystery Epistles, concentrating first on 1 Timothy 3, then drawing on chapters 1, 4 and 6. Parallels from the other Pastoral Epistles will also prove profitable, as will foundational truth from Ephesians and Colossians.

A Good Conscience Concerning the Mystery

Holding fast Christ the Head (Colossians 2:19) may have a doctrinal echo in the ministerial requirements of 1 Timothy 3.

> An overseer then must be blameless ... *holding the mystery of the faith* with a pure conscience. (1 Timothy 3:2, 9)

By its nearness in context, "the mystery of the faith" in verse nine must affect our understanding of "the mystery of godliness" in verse sixteen.

Many are the secrets which God has revealed in His word, and the secrets of 1 Timothy 3:9 and Colossians 2:2 ("the mystery of God – Christ") may, or may not be identical. Another witness must be found to relate 1 Timothy 3:9 back to the admonitions of Colossians 2, for the rule of "two or three witnesses" will help establish the matter

(Deuteronomy 19:15). The needed link can be provided by a survey of the word "conscience" in the Pastoral Epistles. Its first occurrence in these Epistles is revealing:

> … that you might command some not to teach otherwise, *nor to hold onto myths and endless genealogies*, which cause controversies rather than the dispensation of God which *is* in (or by) *the* faith. Now the goal of the command is love from a pure heart and from a good **conscience** and from an unhypocritical faith, from which some, having missed the mark, have gone astray into empty-talk, desiring to be law-teachers, not understanding – neither what they say, nor concerning what they confidently affirm. But we know that the law is good, if anyone should use it lawfully, knowing this – that law is not laid down for a righteous one, but for lawless and insubordinate *ones*, for ungodly and sinful *ones* … (1 Timothy 1:3-9)

In this example we find a pure heart, good conscience and sincere faith in God's dispensation contrasted with the vain jangling of religious fables and debates – evil fruit of the unlawful (i.e., undispensational) use of Mosaic and other divine law. If we fail to hold onto God's dispensation, we will be apt to hold onto such fables.

Issues concerning law appear to ripple throughout the Pastorals. Divine law must have been given to mankind from Adam onward, or the great flood of Noah's time makes no sense – and after Noah too, else the judgment on Sodom would not have been righteous. Note how Peter declares the deeds of Sodom as "lawless" (*anomos* in 2 Peter 2:8). The law in its moral and retributive aspects still has an application today for governing the ungodly masses of men. But for godly ones to misapply the law in their lives is to exchange godliness for ungodliness. Paul shared this same wisdom with Titus in similar words:

> But keep clear of foolish discussions and genealogies and quarrels and law-fights, for they are unprofitable and worthless. Reject a divisive man after a first and second warning, knowing that such a one has been perverted and sins, being self-condemned. (Titus 3:9-11)

This word on "law-fights" foreshadowed religious controversies to come, many of which were about applying legalistic ordinances to a church. All such contentious inquiries into earthly things have been labeled "foolish" by Him Who made known to us "the mystery of His will" in this dispensation.

If the genealogies mentioned in the last two passages have an incipient Gnosticism in mind, as some commentators suggest (Gnosticism became fully developed about a generation later), then the genealogies would refer to the various levels or "aeons" of the creation, from evil earthly matter at one extreme to the pure indescribable spirit of the Father at the other. Mediating between these extremes was supposed to be a hierarchy of Jehovah, then Jesus Christ, then angels, then men, and finally the lowest forms – animal and plant life. Gnosticism was a scheme to deny men their sure access to the Father through Christ.

More teaching about conscience in Titus parallels 1 Timothy 3, both of which set standards for church leaders:

> ... the overseer must be beyond reproach, as God's steward ... *holding firmly the faithful word* according to the doctrine that he may be able both to encourage by the sound teaching and to rebuke those who contradict. For there are many both insubordinate empty-talkers and mind-deceivers, especially those from the circumcision, who must be muzzled, who overturn whole households for sake of disgraceful gain ... rebuke them cuttingly so that they may be sound in the faith, *not holding onto Jewish myths and commandments of men*, who turn away from the truth. All things are pure to the pure, but to the defiled and unfaithful nothing is pure, but even their mind and **conscience** have been defiled. They profess to know God, but they are renounced by their works, being abominable and rebellious and disqualified for every good work. (Titus 1:7-16)

"Holding firmly the faithful word" above is a direct corollary to "holding the mystery of the faith" in 1 Timothy 3:9. The "faithful word" (or "sound teaching") is the doctrine for stewards of "the dispensation of the mystery" in all its practical out-working. In other words, it is the godly walk prescribed for the church – I would even say "commanded" of the church. To insinuate Judaistic elements into "the mystery of the faith" is to defile both the faith and the consciences of the faithful. Purity in our dispensation, unlike the ritual purity of Mosaic ordinances (the "touch not, taste not, handle not" of Colossians 2:21), means to put absolutely no confidence in things of the flesh (Philippians 3:1-9). However, the history of Christian religion has shown the opposite tendency, substituting shadows for the substance of Christ (Colossians 2:17), even as the Holy Spirit warned in the passage immediately following "the mystery of godliness":

But the Spirit speaks explicitly that in later seasons some will desert the faith, *holding onto deceiving spirits and teachings of demons*, liars in hypocrisy, having cauterized their own **conscience**, hindering to marry, to abstain from foods which God created for reception with thanksgiving by the faithful – even those acknowledging the truth. For every created thing of God is good and nothing to be rejected, being received with thanksgiving, for it is sanctified by the word of God and prayer. Placing these things before the brothers, you will be a good servant of Christ Jesus, feeding on the words of the faith and the good teaching which you have closely followed. But reject the vile and silly myths, and exercise yourself for godliness. (1 Timothy 4:1-7)

Summing up the main points of these texts (and a few others) will help clarify where this is leading.

Things held by faith:

The True	The False
holding the mystery of the faith (1 Ti.3:9)	will desert the faith, holding forth to … teachings of demons (1 Ti.4:1)
confess … the mystery of the godliness (1 Ti.3:15-16)	holding onto myths, endless genealogies (1 Ti.1:4)

the acknowledgement of the mystery of God – Christ (Col.2:2)	
holding fast the Head (Col.2:19)	
hold the pattern of sound words (2 Ti.1:13)	
holding firmly the faithful word (Ti.1:9)	
the dispensation (*oikonomia*) of God which is in faithfulness (1 Tim.1:4)	
steward (*oikonomos*) of God, holding firmly the faithful word (Ti.1:7, 9)	holding onto Jewish myths and commandments of men (Ti.1:14)

Godliness - its corollaries and opposites:

The True	The False
but exercise yourself toward godliness (1 Ti.4:7)	reject the vile, silly myths (1 Ti.4:7)

the teaching according to godliness (1 Ti.6:3)	teach otherwise, not agreeing with sound words (1 Ti.6:3)
	teach otherwise (1 Ti.1:3)
the sound teaching to encourage, rebuke (Ti.1:9)	insubordinate empty-talkers and mind-deceivers, especially those from the circumcision (Ti.1:10)
	teaching what they ought not (Ti.1:11)
rebuke cuttingly, so that they may be sound in the faith (Ti.1:13)	Jewish myths and commandments of men (Ti.1:14)
the mystery of the godliness (1 Ti.3:16)	teachings of demons (1 Ti.4:1)
the things fit for the sound teaching (Ti.2:1)	opposed to the sound teaching (1 Ti.1:10)
sound speech above criticism (Ti.2:8)	not bear with the sound teaching (2 Ti.4:3)

feeding on the words of the faith and the good teaching (1 Ti.4:6)	heap up to themselves teachers, itching the ear (2 Ti.4:3)
godliness with contentment is great gain (1 Ti.6:6)	defrauded of the truth, supposing godliness to be gain (1 Ti.6:5)
press after godliness (1 Ti.6:11)	
all the treasures of the wisdom and knowledge (Col.2:3)	avoid…the falsely-named knowledge (1 Ti.6:20)
present yourself an example of good works in the teaching (Ti.2:7)	
present yourself approved to God … rightly dividing the word of the truth (2 Ti.2:15)	

Matters of conscience:

The True	The False
pure conscience (1 Ti.3:9)	mind and conscience defiled (Ti.1:15)
pure heart, good conscience, unhypocritical faith (1 Ti.1:5)	liars in hypocrisy, cauterized their own conscience (1 Ti.4:2)
all things pure to the pure (Ti.1:15)	defiled, unfaithful: nothing pure (Ti.1:15)
	abominable, rebellious, disqualified (Ti.1:16)
acknowledgement of truth which *is* according to godliness (Ti.1:1)	
reception by the faithful, acknowledging the truth (1 Ti.4:3)	hindering marriage, abstain from foods (1 Ti.4:3)
to come unto acknowledgement of truth (1 Ti.2:4)	never able to come unto acknowledgment of truth (2 Ti.3:7)

for acknowledgement of the mystery of God – Christ (Col.2:2)	

Regulations and Law:

The True	The False
overseership – wanting a good work (1 Ti.3:1)	wanting to be law-teachers (1 Ti.1:7)
lawful use of the law (1 Ti.1:8)	law-fights (Ti.3:9)
	Jewish myths & commandments of men (Ti.1:14)
	the tradition of men … the commandments & teachings of men (Col.2:8, 21)
foods … for reception by the faithful, acknowledging the truth (1 Ti.4:3)	hindering marriage, abstain from foods (1 Ti.4:3)

wiped out the rules (Col.2:14)	the elements of the world, rules (Col.2:8, 20 cp. 'elements' in Gal.4:3,9; Heb.5:12)
the circumcision of Christ (Col.2:11)	
from the circumcision…these alone…a comfort to me (Col.4:11)	deceivers…especially from the circumcision (Ti.1:10)
let not any judge in food, drink, feast, new moon, sabbaths (Col.2:16)	touch not, taste not, handle not (Col.2:21)
shadows vs. substance (Col.2:17)	religion of the angels (Col.2:18)
	self-devised religion, severity to the body (Col.2:23)

Words of Peace and Strife:

The True	The False
quiet and peaceful life in all godliness and dignity (1 Ti.2:2)	controversies (1 Ti.1:4)
Overseer…gentle, not quarrelsome (1 Ti.3:3)	empty-talk (1 Ti.1:6)
	avoid the vile empty-speech (1 Ti.6:20)
	insubordinate empty-talkers, mind-deceivers (Ti.1:10)
	philosophy and empty deceit (Col.2:8)
	sick about debates and word-battles … strife (1 Ti.6:4)
	to word-battle for no value (2 Ti.2:14)
	avoid foolish discussions, genealogies, strifes, law-battles (Ti.3:9)

	the foolish and stupid discussions … they generate fights (2 Ti.2:23)
servant of the Lord must not fight … gentle, apt to teach, patient (2 Ti.2:24)	disciplining those who oppose (2 Ti.2:25)
	divisive, perverted, sinning, self-condemned (Ti.3:10-11)
	contradicters (Ti.1:10)
	who is opposed may be shamed (Ti.2:8)
	constant argumentation of men corrupted in the mind (1 Ti.6:5)

Righteous Ones and Sinners:

The True	The False
law not enacted for righteous … (1 Ti.1:9)	… but for lawless and insubordinate, ungodly and sinful, unholy and vile (1 Ti.1:9)
overseer … not for disgraceful gain (1Ti.3:8; Ti.1:7)	for disgraceful gain (Ti.1:11)
	deny God by the works (Ti.1:16)
denying the ungodliness and the worldly passions (Ti.2:12)	a form of godliness, denying its power (2 Ti.3:5)
	deny the faith, worse than unfaithful (1 Ti.5:8)
lest anyone lead you astray (Col.2:4)	miss the mark, go astray (1 Ti.1:6)
lest anyone take you a spoil (Col.2:8)	miss the mark concerning the faith (1 Ti.6:21)

	miss the mark concerning the truth (2 Ti.2:18)
	overturn whole households (Ti.1:11)
	overturn the faith of some (2 Ti.2:18)
	turn away from the truth (Ti.1:14)
	turn away the ears from the truth (2 Ti.4:4)
	ruin those hearing (2 Ti.2:14)
understand what I say (2 Ti.2:7)	not understand (1 Ti.1:7)
insight in all things (2 Ti.2:7)	
every wisdom and spiritual insight (Col.1:9)	
all wealth of the full assurance of the insight (Col.2:2)	

I draw the following conclusions from the foregoing table. The faith, the godliness doctrine, the sound teaching, and the rightly divided word of truth today are the same body of wisdom, each viewed somewhat differently. The faithful maintain a good (pure) conscience not by following Mosaic Law (ritual purity) but by keeping clear of it. The mystery of the faith and the mystery of the godliness relate to the inner, hidden, Christ-energized life of the believer. The opposite is characterized as demon-doctrine, myth, empty-talk, false knowledge, Jewish purity – abominable, rebellious and worse than unfaithful. The opposition hold onto deceiving spirits rather than the energizing Christ-spirit.

The Narrow Context in 1 Timothy 3

I believe there is sufficient ground for reading "the mystery of the faith" in 1 Timothy 3:9 as equivalent to "the mystery of God" and its associated warnings in Colossians 2. The contextual distance from 1 Timothy 3:9 to verse sixteen is even shorter. The mystery of verse nine lies near the end of a section (vv. 1-13) dealing with qualifications for pastors and ministers of the truth. This is followed (vv. 14-16) by a personal exhortation to the minister Timothy concerning his conduct in the house of God. The references to "mystery" ought to be related somehow.

Paul, the "Hebrew of the Hebrews", tended to follow the Hebrew convention of placing modifiers after nouns ("post-positive" word order), as in the example "the mystery of the faith". But for emphasis he occasionally yielded to the classical Greek style of placing the modifier before the noun. In the Mystery Epistles only 8% of genitive noun modifiers and 9% of prepositional phrase modifiers are pre-positive.

Finding that the mystery of godliness is literally "the *of the godliness* mystery", our attention is arrested. May it have been the Holy Spirit's intention to have us pause and make the connection back to "the mystery of the faith"? If so, "the mystery of the godliness" can be seen as an aspect of "the mystery of the faith". That aspect is the empowering of the church for the godly life - godly according to the standard of this non-covenant dispensation.

The Companion Bible offers a marginal comment which bears upon the context in 3:14-15.

1 Tim.3:15 - "That thou mayest know how thou oughtest (RV how men ought) to behave thyself (or what conduct is incumbent on us) in the house of God which is the church of the living God, the pillar and ground of the truth."

What this is, is shown in the next verse, viz., the 'great secret' concerning Christ Mystical and not Christ Personal.

This great Mystery is the Body of Christ, the house in which God dwells by His Spirit; the assembly of the saints peculiarly belonging to the living God, as purchased with the blood of the everlasting covenant, and this is the pillar and ground - the great foundation pillar of the truth, so specially revealed to Paul to make known among the Gentiles.

I believe this view is essentially correct, with the exception of a covenant of blood being involved. Covenant doctrine is among the "things that differ" (Philippians 1:10) for us today.

Some will object to calling the church "the pillar and ground of the truth", as if to put the church on an equality with Him Who is the Truth. Since punctuation was not in use when the earliest manuscripts were penned, we might punctuate the text differently:

> ... *the* house of God which is *the* church of *the* living God. A pillar and ground (that is, 'foundation' or 'base') of the truth, and confessedly great is the mystery of the godliness ...

But this reading does no justice to the architectural metaphor of "pillar and base", which makes sense only if referring back to the temple of the "house of God". The house of God is the church, the "habitation of God through the Spirit" (Ephesians 2:19-22). Perhaps the most sensible way to punctuate the passage is:

> These things I write to you, hoping to come to you shortly; but if I should delay, so that you may know how you should conduct yourself in God's house, Living God's church, a pillar and base of the truth and confessedly great is the mystery of the godliness; God was manifested in *the* flesh ...

The main point will be more readily seen, if we temporarily remove some subordinate clauses.

> ... so that you may know how ... to

conduct yourself in God's house … a pillar and base of the truth and confessedly great is the mystery of the godliness

Here is the kernel of the passage. The mystery of the godliness is set forth so that believers like Timothy may know how to deport themselves in a church in which each one plays a part in edifying the whole (Ephesians 4:16).

Christ has energized with resurrection power the church which is His body, enabling them to live the godly life. The word "church" is found only in chapter three (verses 5 and 15) of 1 Timothy, confirming it as a topic of great weight here. The building up of the church is in view throughout chapter three.

This interpretation of the mystery of godliness in no way detracts from the deity of Christ, which is readily found in the Pastoral Epistles. Six references to God and four to Jesus Christ as Saviour [6] lead us to conclude that They are the same God, for there can be only one Saviour (Isaiah 43:10-11).

---

[6] 1 Timothy 1:1; 2:3; 4:10; 2 Timothy 1:10; Titus 1:3, 4; 2:10, 13; 3:4, 6.

The Deity of Christ in the Mystery of Godliness

The deity of Christ is a necessary basis for the house of God. The following text from Philippians will help illustrate this.

If, therefore, *there is* any encouragement in Christ, if any consolation of love, if any fellowship of spirit, if any sympathies and compassions, fill up my joy so that you may be minded the same, having the same love, joint-souls, minding the one *thing*. Let there be nothing according to contention nor according to vainglory, but in humility esteeming one another above themselves, everyone not looking out for their own *things*, but also the *things* of everyone else. For let this be minded in you which *was* also in Christ Jesus, Who existing in the form of God esteemed it not robbery to be equal with God, but emptied Himself, having taken *the* form of a slave, having become in *the* likeness of men, and having been found in fashion as a man, He humbled Himself having become obedient up to death, even *the* death of a cross. (Philippians 2:1-8)

Because Christ was also God it makes His example all the more poignant, and it ought to prick our hearts for any "spiritual" pride which we might be clinging to. Christ chose the way of the cross to effect our salvation, in part to give us such an example of humility. Without such a self-sacrificing mind, we would be no different from the rest of the world. Christian humility is a gift to each saint, created by divine workmanship in "the new man" (Ephesians 4:23:24; Colossians 3:10-17). The manifestation of this new man in our lives becomes a testimony of the working of the deity of Christ, Who created us anew. But the new man must be "put on" by each of us, if we are to bear any spiritual fruit in our lives (Ephesians 5:8-9). This can be possible only if we also "put off" the old man of the flesh. Having done this, we will become enabled as obedient servants to do the good works of our salvation.

So that, my beloved, even as you always obeyed, not as in my presence only, but now much rather in my absence, work out your own salvation with fear and trembling. For it is God Who works in you, both to desire and to work according to *His* good-pleasure. (Philippians 2:12-13)

The divine energizing operates on a principle more dynamic than any mere physical force – the resurrection power of Christ. The control of this power by One Who was able to lay down His life and take it up again (John 10:17-18) provides another testimony to the deity of Christ. And it is this deity power of the Chief Cornerstone (Ephesians 2:20) that empowers His church, the edifice of "pillar and base" in-worked as described in the mystery of godliness – "God manifested in flesh."

Wider Contexts in the Pastoral Epistles

A structural arrangement of the central section of 1 Timothy might appear like the diagram on the next page. It represents my attempt to put the mystery of godliness in a tighter context.

A. 3:1 Faithful word for those reaching out to minister

    B. 3:2-5 Moderation in family life and things serving carnal needs

        C. 3:6-13 Pride before falling into condemnation, reproach and snare of the devil … model minister not double-tongued … holding the mystery of the faith in a pure conscience

            D. a) 3:14 These things I write to you …

                b) 3:15-16 Godly conduct: the mystery of godliness manifested in the church … the great mystery confessed

        C. 4:1-2 Some give heed to deceiving spirits … lying hypocrites … having cauterized conscience

    B. 4:3-5 Extremism in attitudes toward marriage and food

        D. a) These things laying before the brothers …

            b) 4:7-8 Godly exercise: the promise of life manifested now … the profane and old wives' fables refused

A. 4:9-10 Faithful word for which Paul and Timothy ministered so diligently

An overview of this arrangement of the text shows admonitions to the faithful in chapter 3 contrasted with warnings about deceivers in chapter 4. The connection between the mystery of godliness in D. 3:15-16 and *D.* 4:7-8 lies at the heart of our inquiry. Both passages encourage a godly conduct in the lives of the faithful, enabled by God's life-giving power. Without the present "quickening" (1 Timothy 6:13; Ephesians 2:5) a godly walk in righteousness would be impossible for us until our resurrection.

But 1 Timothy 4:7-8 shows that a new life begins for us in the present sojourn. The contrast between "the mystery of godliness" in the upper half and "the profane and old-wives fables" (Gk. *muthoi* or 'myths') in the lower is also noteworthy. Although the mystery is given to God's elect house to keep, there is a profane counterfeit also. These are the myth-based substitutes based on legalism and fleshly religion. Over in 2 Timothy 3:5 the myth is described as having a "form of godliness" without power, and it includes all forms and venues that excite religious feelings.

If believers are not well grounded in the word of God, rightly divided, they might become easily stirred by "the spirit of man" (1 Corinthians 2:11 – i.e., their own emotions) or "the prince of the power of the air". On the other hand, the teaching in 1 Timothy 3 revolves around expressions of a powerful godliness, and they become beacons for those who are ambitious to serve.

Chapter six has some interesting correspondences with chapter three and is also important for providing context. In 6:3 we have literally "the *according to godliness* teaching", which is notable for its word order and thematic parallels to "the *of the godliness* mystery".

The expression "the according to godliness *teaching*" answers to "these things *teach* and encourage" in 6:2. An extension of this teaching in 6:6, "godliness with contentment is *great gain*", seems to answer both the "*good degree*" acquired by those who serve well (3:13) and "the godliness … *profitable* for all things" (4:8). The gain and the mystery are both described as "great".

The deeds of "men of the corrupted mind" (6:5) are opposed to the "blameless" practices (3:2) of the model man of God. Timothy "*confessed* the good *confession*" (6:12), while the mystery of godliness is called "*confessedly* great". The "God Who *makes alive*" (6:15) is also the "*living* God" (3:16). A "good *foundation*" of deeds by those who are "rich in good works" (6:18-19) is necessary for building up "the *house* of God ... church of the living God, the *pillar and ground* of the truth" (3:15). The "good teaching" closely followed (4:6-7) and the "deposit" kept (6:20) are contrasted with profane fables and babblings in both sections.

The following structural analysis, summing up the whole of 1 Timothy, is taken from an article by Charles Welch [7] on the mystery of godliness:

---

[7] *Alphabetical Analysis*, Charles Welch, part 3, p. 93.

A. 1:17 The King of the Ages, Incorruptible, *invisible*. Honour and glory, to the ages of the ages.

B. 3:16 God was manifested in the flesh. *Seen*.

A. 6:16 King of kings, Immortal, *Unseen*, Honour and might, age-lasting.

Mr. Welch's zeal in defending the deity of Christ is admirable. However, he himself took exception to the use of another popular proof text of Christ's divinity:

> For in Him dwells all the fullness of deity bodily. And you are filled in Him, Who is the Head. (Colossians 2:9-10)

He explained [8]:

> Those of us who believe the doctrine of the Deity of Christ naturally turn to Colossians 2:9 as to a proof text, but this may not be the right attitude of heart and mind when dealing with the Sacred Scriptures. We do no honour to the

---

[8] ibid., part 3, p. 249.

Lord, if we misuse a portion of Scripture, even to "prove" or to enforce the glorious doctrine of His Deity. *Truth needs no bolster.*

These are points that I would apply to 1 Timothy 3:16 being used as a proof text of the deity of Christ. While Welch applied "God was manifested in the flesh" to Christ in His person, I would apply it to the body of Christ. The outer members of his structure (**A**, *A*) both refer to the kingship of Christ. The heavenly kingdom with Christ already seated there in glory (Ephesians1:18-20) is an aspect of the overall kingdom of God which for the present is unseen by us and unapproachable for us in bodily terms.

However, at "the appearing of our Lord Jesus Christ" (1 Timothy 6:14), that which was hidden concerning the King will be manifested to His church in resurrection (Colossians 3:4). Although the full glory of that heavenly kingdom remains veiled until the future, some of its glory is manifest even now through a church described as "translated into the kingdom of His dear Son" (Colossians 1:13). In the personal absence of the

King, the church is the very evidence that this kingdom is operating in the earth today.

By walking as "children of light", the light of Christ emanates from us, and this can be both seen and approached. The "church which is His body" is called His fullness (Ephesians 1:23), even as Christ dwelling in (or among) the church is called "the mystery" (Colossians 1:26-27). This is certainly a sense in which we may understand "God was manifested in the flesh". And identifying itself as part of "the mystery of godliness" helps align this truth with aspects of the mystery revealed in Ephesians and Colossians. 1 Timothy, then, is very much truth for today.

There is an even larger structure across the two Timothy Epistles (next page), that includes at its core Mr. Welch's structure. It expands on the theme of King and kingdom, and this attempt to find a contextual pattern is more detailed. The four sections labelled "**A**" are linked by references to kingship and kingdom (in bold font). Each half has a central member (**B**) drawing attention to the believer's participation in the kingdom of Christ.

The earlier "**A**" pair in 1 Timothy emphasizes the majesty of Christ in a doxology. The latter pair in 2 Timothy deal with Christ as Judge of His servants.

The central "**B**" sections provide truths about the church's practical involvement in the mystery of the faith. Godly conduct must include dispensationally correct (that is, "rightly divided") conduct. These two aspects of the believer's life-work are mirrored in Ephesians 5 in the "walk as children of light" and "walk circumspectly" (literally, "accurately").

Appendix A offers a contextual pattern of all three Pastoral Epistles based on the word "godliness". Here the "mystery of godliness" stands in sharp contrast with "a form of godliness" without divine power. But "the mystery of godliness ... God manifested in the flesh" has divine power.

Heavenly Kingdom in the Timothy Epistles

A. 1 Timothy 1:11-17

   a) "if any other thing is opposed to the sound teaching"

     b) "according to the gospel of the glory of the happy God" given to Paul

       c) formerly a persecutor, "but the grace of God super-abounded"

         d) faithful word: "Christ Jesus came into the world to save sinners"

           e) of whom Paul was first, "a pattern of those about to believe on Him for life eternal … to **the King of the ages** be honor and glory for the ages of the ages. Amen."

B. 3:15-16

           f) "how it behooves one to conduct himself in God's house"

           g) the mystery of godliness: foundation of the truth and confessedly great

A. 6:12-16

   h) "fight the good fight of the faith"

     i) "lay hold of the eternal life for which you were called and did confess the good confession before many witnesses"

j) "I charge you before God, Who preserves all these alive, and Christ Jesus Who witnessed … the good confession, that you keep the command spotless and irreproachable until the appearing of our Lord Jesus Christ, which in its own seasons will show the happy and only Potentate, the **King of kings** and Lord of lords … to Whom be honor and eternal might. Amen."

A. *2 Timothy 2:8-13*

  d) Remember: Jesus Christ … came into the world from David's seed … raised for us

b) "according to my gospel"

  c) Paul was persecuted, "but the word of God was not bound"

    e) Paul endured all things for the elect's sake, that they might obtain the salvation in Christ Jesus with eternal glory. Faithful word: death and life with Him; endurers will also **reign with the King**; deniers will be denied the crown

B. *2:15*

  f) "be diligent to present yourself approved to God, an unashamed workman"

g) (professing the mystery) by "rightly dividing the word of truth"

A. 4:1-8, 18

    j) "I earnestly testify before God and Christ Jesus, Who is about to judge living and dead according to **His** appearing and **kingdom**, proclaim the word

a) "a season when they will not bear the sound teaching"

    i) "be sober … suffer evil, do an evangelist's work, fulfil your ministry"

h) "I have fought the good fight, I have finished the course, I have kept the faith"

    j) the Lord the righteous Judge, will render the crown in the day of His appearing. "the Lord … will preserve me for **His heavenly kingdom**; to Whom be glory to the ages of the ages. Amen."

The Mystery of Godliness in Its Six Parts

Several lines of thought connect the mystery of godliness with the mystery teaching of Ephesians, particularly chapter 5. These are the only two places in Scripture where a mystery is called "great".

> This is a **great mystery**, but I speak as to Christ and the church. (Ephesians 5:32)

> And confessedly **great** is **the mystery** of godliness … (1 Timothy 3:16)

The "great mystery" of Ephesians 5:32 is explained in verses 28-31.

> So ought the husbands to love their wives as their own bodies. He that loves his own wife loves himself. For no one ever hated his own flesh, but feeds and takes care of it, even as also Christ *does* the church, because we are members of His body. Because of this a man will leave behind his father and his mother and will be united with his wife, and the two will be for one flesh.

Comparing Christ and church to a husband and wife, joined as one flesh corresponds to the first element of the mystery of godliness – its being "manifested in the flesh". After His resurrection the Lord made a point to demonstrate that He was no disembodied spirit, but had a body of "flesh and bones" (Luke 24:36-43). As members of His body, we have been joined to Christ, and His power and spirit have come to dwell in us. The "Light of the world" (John 8:12) has shone upon us, so that we have become "light in the Lord" (Ephesians 5:8, 13-14).

The second part of the mystery of godliness, "justified in spirit", is the subject of Ephesians 5:25-27.

Husbands love your wives, even as Christ also loved the church and gave Himself for it, so that He might sanctify it, having cleansed *it* with the washing of the water by word, so that He might present it to Himself the glorious church, not having blemish or wrinkle or any such things, but that it might be holy and faultless.

Being cleansed and made faultless are facets of being justified by Him, by the one (spiritual) baptism that washed us (Ephesians 4:5). This must be accomplished "in spirit" because no good thing dwells in the flesh (Romans 7:18). This text also touches on the sixth element of the mystery of godliness, "received up in glory". A more literal rendering of Ephesians 5:27 would be: "that He might present the *inglory* church to Himself." This refers not to the future glory of Colossians 3:4, but to a present glory – the state of a church spiritually co-seated in the heavenlies in Christ (Ephesians 1:3-4, 18-22; 2:4-6).

The third item of the mystery of godliness, "seen of angels", concerns the relationship of the body of Christ to the principalities and powers in the heavenlies. In harmony with God's purpose of the ages, we are demonstrating to them His manifold wisdom (Ephesians 3:10-11). In this same light, Paul charged Timothy "before God and Christ Jesus and the chosen angels" (1 Timothy 5:21). I often look for the unusual expressions in Scripture – they bear the mark of the Holy Spirit's exclamation point, as it were. This is one such expression, "the chosen (or elect) angels". A contest between good and bad angels, and between bad angels and God, can be glimpsed occasionally in the OT, and a great battle between these groups awaits a future time (Revelation 12:7). In the current dispensation we are drawn into the very center of spiritual conflict with the bad angels, singularly described as "the world-rulers of this darkness, against the spiritual things of the wickedness in the heavenlies" (Ephesians 6:12). Paul's calling on Father, Son and chosen angels to witness his charge to Timothy puts those angels on our team, although their only deed for the present is to be witnesses of the words and deeds of elect men.

The fourth expression of the mystery of godliness, "proclaimed among the nations" describes the uniquely nation-ward dispensation of God's grace (Ephesians 3:1-2, 6; Colossians 1:27). The Israelite is not excluded from taking part, but he must do so apart from any covenant privileges of the past.

The fifth part, "believed in the world", indicates that faith is the necessary first step for a godly walk. We are not able of ourselves to live godly, but by divine workmanship godly lives have been prepared for us (Ephesians 2:8-10). Some context in 1 Timothy 1:15-16 speaks of faith coming into the world, with Paul declaring himself the pattern – the first to believe. Although he casts a look back to his conversion experience in Acts chapter 9 (1:12-13), Paul was a latecomer to believe in Jesus as the hope of Israel.

Some prefer to translate "foremost to believe" of Paul the pattern, so Paul's statement is open to diverse interpretations. However, the text has some unique expressions. For example, "the gospel of the glory of the happy God", which I discussed earlier, is a unique expression of the gospel. Paul also calls himself "a proclaimer and apostle … teacher of nations" (2:7, also 2 Timothy 1:11) in that ministry which was given him. He is no longer just "apostle of nations" (Romans 11:13), but also their teacher. In a sense he was also "first to believe" in this dispensation of the grace of God, because to him was given the revelation of the great mystery concerning heavenly places as our place of blessing.

The use of numbers in the Bible is not without

significance. Six is the number of man and things suited to his use.[9] Like the six-sided exampleship for believers in 1 Timothy 4:12, and the six-fold pursuit of 1 Timothy 6:11, the six parts of the mystery of godliness indicate that it is man-ward rather than God-ward truth. Note the correlation with the Spirit's dire warning that follows, also in six parts:

1) later on some will desert the faith,
2) paying heed to deceiving spirits,
3) lying in hypocrisy,
4) cauterized in their conscience,
5) forbidding to marry,
6) *bidding* to abstain from foods.[10]

---

[9] More on the Biblical significance of the number 6 will be found in *Number in Scripture*, E.W. Bullinger, pp. 150-157.

[10] Add to these the six implements of the panoply of God in Ephesians 6:13-17, the six types of building material in 1 Corinthians 3:12, and the six "whatsoevers" for the faithful in Philippians 4:8.

Conclusion

Conclusion

This discussion of the mystery of godliness has attempted to show the rich context of the subject. Although my interpretation differs from the standard one, it does depend on the doctrinal foundation of the deity of Christ. I believe it even corroborates His deity. Without "all the fullness of the deity" in Christ, how could His body the church be filled with anything at all? It is only in Christ that the church has received "every spiritual blessing in the heavenlies" – God's increase has become our increase through Christ Jesus.

The bulk of 1 Timothy and its companion Pastoral Epistles are devoted to practical teaching. Much instruction is given to individual ministers like Timothy, and the pastors he appointed in local churches. The tone of the Pastoral Epistles is very personal, and gets down to cases – good and bad. Doubtless, Timothy and Titus were well versed in the doctrines of the great mystery of Ephesians and Colossians. What they needed now from a fatherly Paul was not so much the doctrine, but the reproof, the correction and the discipline in righteousness that makes the man of God complete (2 Timothy 3:15-17). The few statements of fundamental teaching in the Pastorals were not given to lay again the foundation of Christ, but to encourage these younger men of God. Shortly they would be required to stand alone in their faith, without the elder Paul to guide them.

In this time of sectarian Christianity, one must decide whether a teacher is to be heard based on his word and his walk. The touchstone of all teaching and practice in the body of Christ must be founded upon the word of truth – diligently searched and rightly divided. Having done this, we may trust in the Lord to fill up what is lacking in us. The goal is spiritual maturity - to be "grown into Him in all things, Who is the Head, even Christ" (Ephesians 4:15). In working out this knowledge, we should be seeking a life of godly conduct, whose operation is summed up in "the mystery of godliness".

Appendix A: Godliness in the Pastoral Epistles

Appendix A: Godliness in the Pastoral Epistles

A^1.	1 Tim 2:2	that we may lead a tranquil life in all **godliness** and dignity
B.	3:15-16	confessedly great is the mystery of **godliness**: God was manifested in flesh (of His saints, that is) ...
C.a.	4:7	exercise yourself as to **godliness**
b.	4:8	for bodily exercise is profitable for a little while, but **godliness** is profitable for everything
D.	6:3	sound words ... of our Lord Jesus Christ, even the teaching according to **godliness**
C.a.	6:5	men ... destitute of truth, holding **godliness** to be gain
b.	6:6	but **godliness** with contentment is great tain
A^2.	6:11	flee these things and pursue

		righteousness, **godliness**, faith, love
B.	2 Timothy 3:5	having a form of **godliness** but denying the power of it
A¹.	3:12	all who want to live **godly** in Christ Jesus will be pressured
D.	Titus 1:1	recognition of truth which is according to **godliness**
A².	2:12	having denied ungodliness and worldly passions we should live discreetly and righteously and **godly** in the present age

Summary

A1 Quiet life in godliness to be desired, but godly life in conflict rather to be expected.

B The mystery of godliness (in-worked power) contrasted with the mystery of iniquity (power denied)
The profit or gain of godliness contrasted with the profit of the flesh.

D Teaching or truth which is "according to godliness"

A2 Flee the old life of sin and pursue the new life that is righteous and godly.

About the Author

Glen Burch was born in Washington, D.C., in 1947, and is at present enjoying retirement in Virginia where he is a teacher at Grace Bible Church of Hampton Roads. After high school, and his time in the army, he held several positions before becoming a civilian analyst with the U.S. Navy, a position he held for many years.

Also by Glen Burch

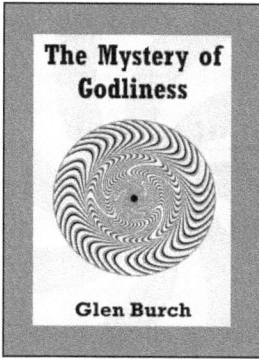

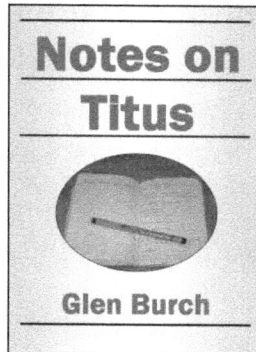

The Mystery of Godliness

Tithing and other gifts

Abraham's Progress in the Covenant of God

Notes on Titus

Please note:

Further details of all the books mentioned can be
seen on **www.obt.org.uk**

The can be ordered from the website
and also from

The Open Bible Trust,
Fordland Mount, Upper Basildon,
Reading, RG8 8LU, UK.

They are also available as eBooks
from Amazon and Apple,
and also as KDP paperbacks from Amazon.

Search Magazine

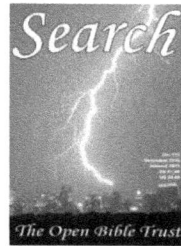

For a free sample of
The Open Bible Trust's magazine Search,
please email

admin@obt.org.uk

or visit

www.obt.org.uk/search

About this Book

The Mystery of Godliness

Most commentators hold the view that the mystery of godliness, spoken of in 1 Timothy 3:16, refers to Christ personal and as such it has been one of the proof texts for His deity.

Glen Burch avidly supports the scriptural testimony concerning the deity of the Lord Jesus Christ but he is of the view that in 1 Timothy 3:16 Paul was writing about Christ mystical, the Church which is His Body. What the author says is worthy of much consideration.

www.ingramcontent.com/pod-product-compliance
Lightning Source LLC
Chambersburg PA
CBHW070529030426
42337CB00016B/2164